Print Edition ISBN: 978-1-0688499-0-9.
Digital Edition ISBN: 978-1-0688499-1-6

Concept by Gail Gatt
Art by Christopher Gatt
Graphic Design by Max Gatt

Apple

2
B
ugs

3

4

Doughnuts

6
Fish

7
Girrafes

8
Hot dogs

9
ce cream
cones

10

Jelly
beans

11
Kittens

12
ollipops

13

Marbles

14

15
Oranges

16
Penguins

17
Quarters

18
Radishes

19
S
un-
flowers

20
T
urtles

21
Umbrellas

22
Vases

23
W
hales

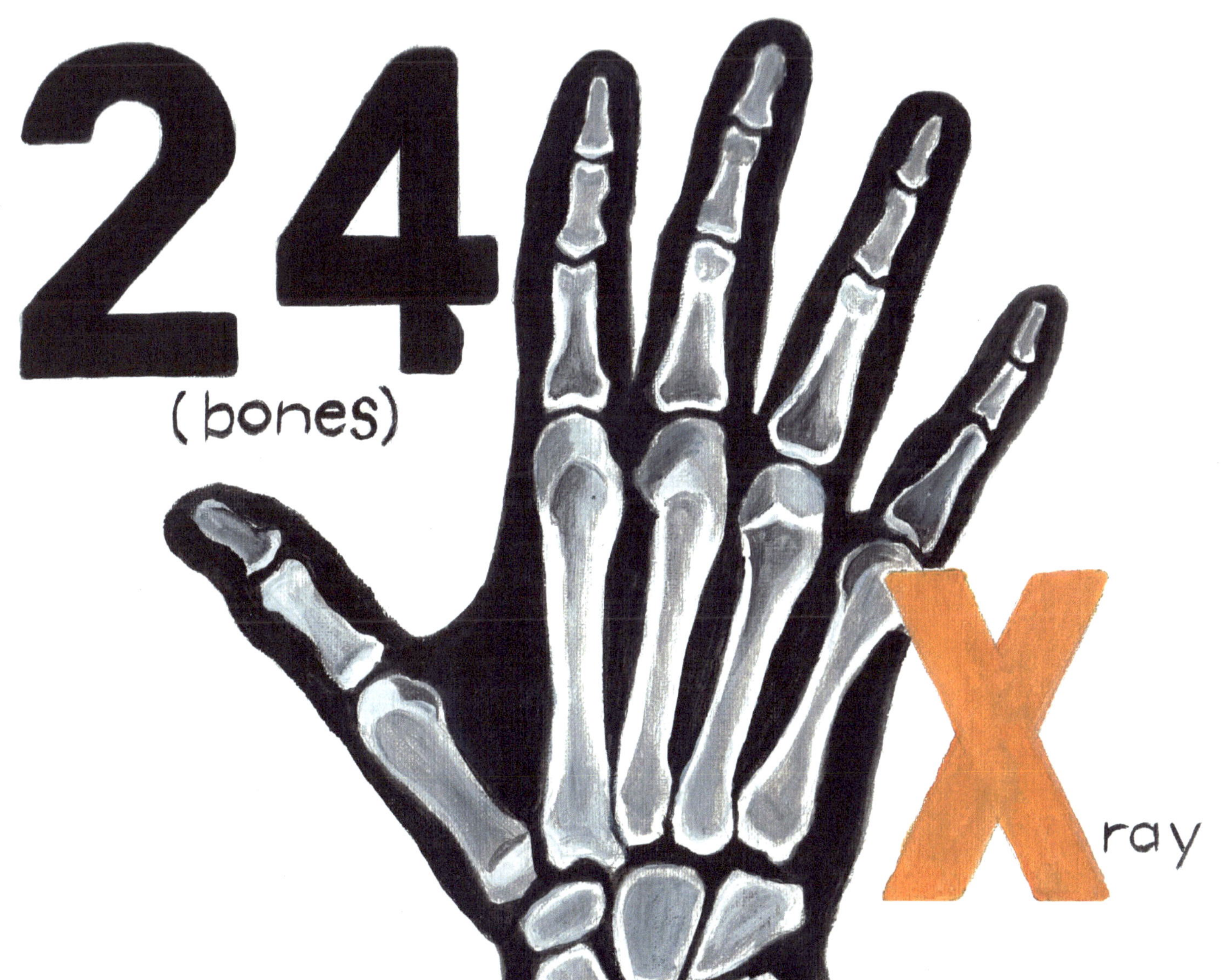

24
(bones)
X ray

25
Y
oyos

26
Zucchini